DEATH IS THE PLACE

POEMS BY
WILLIAM
BRONK

NORTH POINT PRESS

San Francisco 1989

LIBRARY OF CONGRESS CATALOGING-IN-PUBLICATION DATA
Bronk, William.
   Death is the place : poems / by William Bronk.
      p. cm.
   ISBN 0-86547-409-5
   I. Title.
PS3552.R65D4   1989
811'.54— dc20   89-8577

CONTENTS

3   The Time Observed

4   Dawnings

5   Later

6   Things Going Bump

7   How It Diminishes Us

8   Caretaker

9   Its Contempt

10   Real Thinking

11   The License

12   Question Put To

13   The Automobile Age

14   Coming Up Short

15   Real Estate

16   Adversaries

17   Of Poetry

18   Deaf Beethoven

19   Emptying Out

20   The Mind's Dispossession

21   Perspective

22   Vicarious

23   The Fiction of Real

24   Special Olympics

25   All in the Family

26   At Last

27   Praeludium

28   Mundane

29   Has Been

30   Holy Ghost

31 The Import-Export Ratio

32 May Card

33 The Unified Force

34 Image and Likeness

35 Somebody Wolff Knew

36 Look What's Talking

37 At Four in the Morning

38 Private Line

39 To Be

40 Real Loss

41 Look Under

42 Overnight

43 Room for a View

44 Worksong

45 Housing the Homeless

46 Post-Mortem

47 Fostering

48 Faults and Vicinities

49 Elder Brother

50 Matins

DEATH IS THE PLACE

THE TIME OBSERVED

Death is the place I want to go to
again. Not now. Not yet awhile. But I'm sure
it's there. The days and nights observe this.

DAWNINGS

Summers, dawn says the dark is aberrant
but in winter, dawn's confidence astonishes
coming with all it knows about the dark.

LATER

When I was little the lights in the natural world
were not so beautiful as they are now.
No worry. They'll still be there. I know.

THINGS GOING BUMP

Wind-noise of the house all night in the fall:
dreaded. But in spring the noise an elation. Come on!

HOW IT DIMINISHES US

What happens to man is his happening
upon some other happening
which hadn't to do with him he'd thought, as if
some distance off—much as astral occurrence, say,
but here, and he not even happening.

CARETAKER

I keep the house of course and what it holds
not that I care now. But I care.
I know I can't save it or save myself
but, passers in a passing place, and while we last
what else? Where things are done there's nothing for us
to do but watch it done. Be proud and play.

ITS CONTEMPT

Art doesn't need us, stands complete
in cold contempt for us. Sure it will
take our money—any currency—jewels
—real or fake—indifferent; it doesn't care.
And time: whatever time no matter; you won't
get art with time. Art takes everything,
gives nothing. The devotion we get to keep
is our own, the one that with pride we had to bring.

REAL THINKING

Reality is willing we should think
about it: no harm. But it isn't going to be
comprehended by our thought or even admit
to us its being there. "Maybe I'm not,"
it says. Ha, ha; funny type.
Meanwhile, we doubt ourselves, too, as far
as thinking goes, finding us just as strange,
finding us both not any way possible.

THE LICENSE

Summer is the deepness of trees. I am won
by the wonder. Riches. Splendor. The tree itself
fruit I feast on. I am unforbidden.

QUESTION PUT TO

How many times is needed the assurance then
of the ecstasy of the world—*yes, oh yes*—
before there be *let go* and we be gone?

THE AUTOMOBILE AGE

Toward the end, the scare isn't death but life
which had seemed, as we say, a car we drove
or rode in; but now the car—used—
is cannibalized in the auto junk-yard
and hadn't been going anywhere anyway.

COMING UP SHORT

The way God said *light* man
said *time*, said *space* and there they were.
What else but the stars could cause the saying, what else
is grand enough? But if stars are what they thought
to deal with, intimidated at first,
they didn't dare. They tried them out on things
like lives, they measured lands, made clocks
and calendars and saw they worked, then
dared the stars, saw time make space
to their surprise and they were pleased with this
but it wasn't all: it needed something else.
It had been almost right, almost enough.

REAL ESTATE

You know, when we first came here
these houses were all empty. Some of us made
them, after a fashion, livable again
but, as you can see, there are parts we don't use
and pieces we've added on or taken off,
rooms we've divided, things like that to try
to suit us more. You need a permit but some of us
go ahead anyway.
                    Those houses there
were just put up. They weren't here.
People find that easier.
I think it's wrong and, up back, there are more
houses like this, roofs good,
walls solid, dark maybe and strange,
brush and trees around but even so,
vacant to be had. You know, I wonder who
it was that built them. They weren't like us.

15

ADVERSARIES

The brother
who fights
his brother
may kill
his brother
or be killed
by him.

So?

The eternal father
stays.

OF POETRY

there is only the work.

The work is what speaks
and what is spoken
and what attends to hear
what is spoken.

DEAF BEETHOVEN

Terrible things will happen to us even as
we hold each other to hold them off even as,
elsewhere, atoms disintegrate and stars
explode and neither are they of consequence
to what really happens without we know
if it does or how, the real unmodified
and deaf to what the deaf Beethoven heard.

EMPTYING OUT

How it is like the first day now
—the bareness between the evening and the morning which were
the first day.
                Winter now and light
comes late and it is celebrant
and just the light is enough, the idea of light,
the waking naked to it. Then evening coming on
and the memory of light in the eased dark
and nakedness again, the lying down.

THE MIND'S DISPOSSESSION

Asleep, the mind, too, has gravities.
Coherent: dreams of falling terrorize
and we wake in gratitude to the bed, the floor,
the under earth, accustomed solidities
the body owns and only the body; the mind
wakes to its natural weightlessness
and reaches out to some weak mass
of its devising and leans there, wide awake.

PERSPECTIVE

We have always been docile and obedient
without even knowing we were. We thought the voice
we heeded was ours and it mattered. We admired our acts
of decision, our weightings of goodness and wickednesses
or supposed there were victims of personal forces called fate.

But cathedrals built and they used us the way they used stones.
And wars divided the undecided to sides
and awarded, indifferently, deaths and wealth and powers
where none of these dramas were even what really went on
if something did: we don't even know if it did.

VICARIOUS

Except from our
mortality
how should
infinite
eternal know
how beautiful
the brief world
is to us?

THE FICTION OF REAL

The false roles we play are a way to rid
ourselves of falsity and be real in a real
world as we need to be to realize
our potential. There is where the action is
and inaction is wrong. The need is for faith
and vision and, unless we believe, our fiction falls
and we with it, our civilization ends.

SPECIAL OLYMPICS

Almost everything is different in the world
of fun and conflict. It's a game world
and the rules are all made up but you learn the moves
and how to use them—the smart guys even change
them as they go along. It's a test of strength and skill
and almost everybody can play. There are jobs
and promotions and there isn't a limit to what you can win
—lotteries even and what the world calls
dominion,—be king of the hill. True, you can lose.

ALL IN THE FAMILY

The I is like the eye: it watches while
the mind and body do things on their own.
Quite often out of sight, they come up with surprises—
                                        to themselves
as much as the I. Willful, like kids, they take
stupid chances, they quarrel and conspire, get smart,
learn a little, win the I with their charm
but show scant affection back. Even the help
they give seems less compassion than a boast.
And don't they mean to destroy the I in the end?

AT LAST

Not asking for mercy
or stating,
I stand
in a presence.

PRAELUDIUM

The face that, mornings, shows itself for wash
and shave knows more than the spurious terrors of night.
Its eyes show shots it doesn't need to have seen
and lines walked deep in the skin go nowhere again.
What, in the drooped mouth, can balk its mutter?
Nothing. Let the water run to warm.

MUNDANE

What we do gets so natural
feels so good to us
we forget what we are
and any interruption,
lessening,
even the final breaking off
seems terrible
and wrong.

HAS BEEN

It used to take time—ten years,
twenty—for a now to glaze over, age
itself into a harmless then. Now,
in my mild years, it comes with the glaze on.

HOLY GHOST

In the feel of desire
he becomes so real
we have written him books
and built him houses.
Times that he comes
we can hear him read.

THE IMPORT-EXPORT RATIO

Was he the father or the son? We mix up
generations and people of the same name
not any way related. We do know
(are pretty sure) this family married
that one but forget which one was the bride and which
the groom. It was important.

                                      Our pleasures, too;
we can take pleasure in the most austere self-
denial or gross indulgence and be proud with the same
pride in either pleasure. Where is the pride
when it's gone? The things that mattered never did.
Inside, there's nothing to hold on to.

MAY CARD

When I woke up, all outside
was a light green fog, a window full
and it was the ginkgo out in little leaves.

THE UNIFIED FORCE

The force from fathers that sons fight against
or for is one force and the sons' force.

All the energy of the universe
is allied and breaks alliance to fight
itself and wonders, watches, serene with hurt.

IMAGE AND LIKENESS

They have been thought to be Gods and Goddesses
and, feeling power, we have entreated them
—strengths we knew such as sun and moon are
or how wars come or crops grow—
should they, in their turn, know us as it seemed they should
for all their bearing, seeming intention, on us.
How should we not have thought they saw and heard?

And their beauty, too: it awed us to be around
them, our lives in their sanctuary, even if they not
know us, didn't see, didn't hear.
We saw sacrament as much as if we,
ourselves, were God—our meager selves
we barely understood, dark source,
dark ending, doubtful power, suffering,
having to be and having to be ourselves.

SOMEBODY WOLFF KNEW

We done a lot of work before we come here
and it was good work too but not I guess
in any place important, kind of off
in the edges. Not that this place is much
either and I couldn't do it now anyway but I
wonder where the real work was and who
did it. Somebody musta. Maybe nobody did.

LOOK WHAT'S TALKING

It isn't what we say of reality
is metaphor but reality itself
which is. Reality as God or as
cosmos or as, more often, both at once
—whatever—reality is metaphor
not more not less and, being that,
is real as can be and not quite real:

always brilliantly true and less than whole.

AT FOUR IN THE MORNING

Poetry wasn't all. In some degree
I found what others find
is enough to live for that might be still
enough if there isn't some more that's left to say.

PRIVATE LINE

In the act of love we call upon that God
who commands the call and need not answer us.
As if we needed answer, we call, and call.

TO BE

old is
to be
driven by
quick-tiring drives
that keep sleep from
sleeping away
the tirednesses.

REAL LOSS

If I think the actual is real I think to look
for a life after death or even before death
actual as this one is but, of course,
better than this—a bettered actual—
disclaiming real, having instead of it.

LOOK UNDER

In some sleeps
I'm under dirt
and held there
feel
the weight of it.

Not dreaming
I hold
to one thought
search earth
untold
untelling
search earth.

OVERNIGHT

Even the house. Up early, I look
at it in the half dark and sense its own
selfness. Puzzling: the wooden remote of my old
familiar. Its grace and kindness remembered were just
that I stayed there. I could have been anybody
and I'll be checking out. Vacancy.

The world outside even more. The much
I may have loved it it wasn't mine.
There it is. It hadn't to do with me.

ROOM FOR A VIEW

From space, the whole earth shows so small
—pet to gentle the hand or speck to swat
fly-like, as who should ever know or care?

WORKSONG

The little we know or do doesn't make the form
and nature of things. The form and nature of things
is something we'll never know. How shall we show
our respect for something we'll never know? Let it be
in the nature and form of that little we know and do.

HOUSING THE HOMELESS

We are here like castaways from who knows where.
And who knows where is here? Whoever here
is human is who we are; so whom to ask?

But we know it isn't ours—so huge and we
too clumsy, too, for its tininesses. We find
places where our wrong size seems
to fit or make some place our
size to defy uneasiness and it
is the here and we have it to make the best of.

Or else, concede the great disparities,
alienate to them a property
not ours to claim, let them humble us,
homeless, in ungrudged place in their spacious world,
housed in the wonder of it and comforted.

POST-MORTEM

When I go to bed I go, so to say, backstage
where the play is over, the curtain drawn and no
more story to be told. I want to look at what
machinery gave the illusions, what props and lights
and who the actors were, walk around,
finger things. Of course, we were fooled
but sleep will tell me what the powerful
magic was, sleep will show me the book
and let me read the language for myself.

FOSTERING
for Ed Foster

Ed asks me
does the poem depend
on what is said
or language saying

but the poems are
acts of love:

they depend.

FAULTS AND VICINITIES

The regardless of stars, we gaze yet at them.

The crusts of the earth move with mountainous slowness and power.

They seem to be firm. Our quick lives quit from their edges.

ELDER BROTHER

Death is the one immortal, he that
fraternal *in utero*, born again
with each of us when we are born yet old
already, older than anything and death
will be chief of mourners to mourn our dying, death
is our guide and we quarrel and argue against him but thin
the life without his ready company.

MATINS

Early, before the day has been, I know
the day. I lie with it in the unspoken dark.
Sometimes, I doze again to mark its coming.

Design by David Bullen
Typeset in Mergenthaler Imprint
with Meridien display
by Wilsted & Taylor
Printed by Malloy Lithographing
on acid-free paper